Simple experiments with a ball which will teach you to observe and reason on the basis of your observations.

Adventures with a Ball

D1505832

Another book of First Science Experiments

By HARRY MILGROM

Adventures with a String

adventures with a ball
first science experiments

by Harry Milgrom

illustrated by the strimbans

E. P. DUTTON & CO., INC.
NEW YORK

Siskiyou County Schools Library
E.S.E.A. TITLE II, PHASE TWO, 1969

TO MY GRANDSON
Jerrold Scot Milgrom
and all the other inquisitive children
of his generation whose nimble minds
will help fathom more and more of the
unsolved mysteries of the universe
in which they dwell.

Published simultaneously in Canada by Clarke,
Irwin & Company Limited, Toronto and Vancouver

Library of Congress Catalog Card Number: 65-21288

Adventures with a Ball

A ball is an interesting thing.

Get a soft ball.

What is the shape of the ball?

Put the ball into a glass.

The ball fits the glass.   Put a dot on the ball.

6

Turn the ball many ways.

Does the ball fit the glass each way?

A thing that fits all ways is round.

The ball is round.

The ball is a sphere.

Does a block fit all ways?

Is a block round?

Is a block a sphere?

Does a doll fit all ways?

Is a doll round?

Is a doll a sphere?

Use a glass to find out.

Squeeze the ball.

What happens to the shape of the ball?

The ball does not stay round.

Let go.

What happens?

9

How big is the ball across? How would you find out?

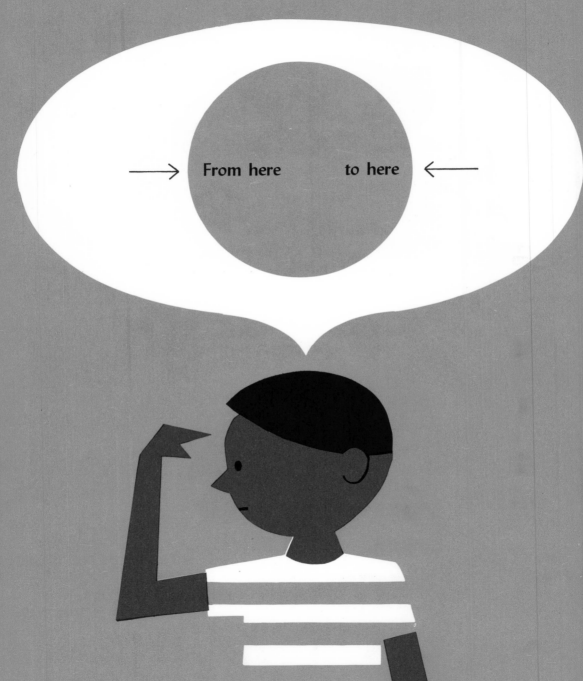

Put the ball between two blocks.

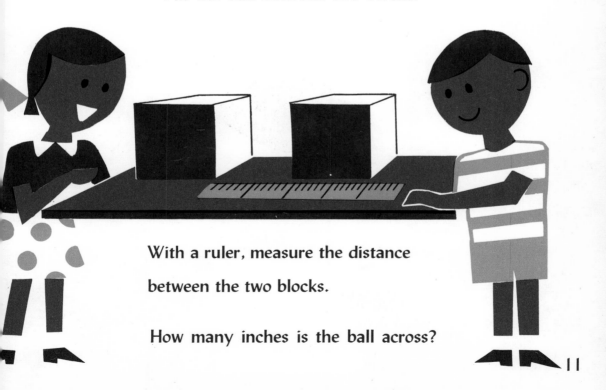

With a ruler, measure the distance

between the two blocks.

How many inches is the ball across?

11

How far around is the ball? How would you find out?

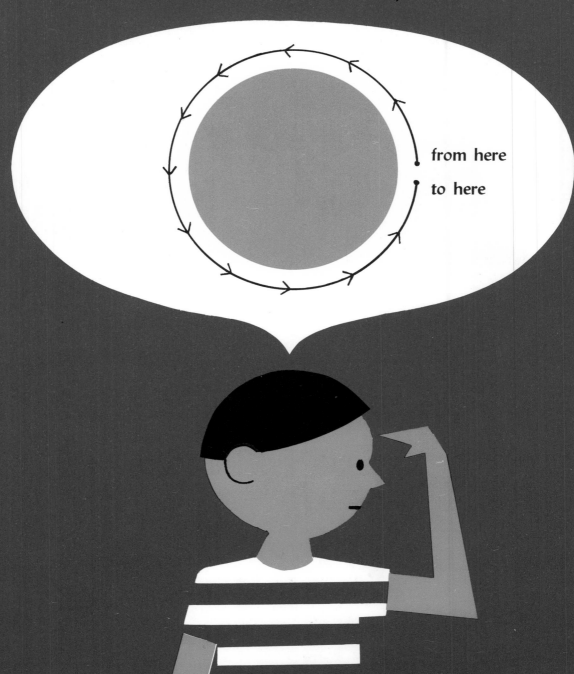

from here
to here

Wrap a string around the ball.

Hold the place where the string comes back to the start.

Unwrap the string.

Measure it with a ruler.

How many inches is the ball around?

Is the ball bigger across or around?

Put the ball in sunlight.

How large is the ball's shadow?

What is the shape of the ball's shadow?

The ball's shadow is larger than the ball.

The ball's shadow has a different shape than the ball.

Hold the ball near the top of a table.

Let go of the ball.

What happens to the ball?

The ball bounces.

It does not bounce up to the top of the table.

It does not bounce as high as it was.

Drop the ball from the top of the table again.

How many times does the ball bounce?

How high is each bounce?

The ball bounces many times.

Each bounce is not as high as the one before.

The last bounces are hard to see.

Drop the ball on a carpet.

Drop the ball on a wooden floor.

Does the ball bounce higher on the carpet or the wooden floor?

The ball bounces higher on the wooden floor.

Why do you think the ball bounces

higher on the wooden floor than on the carpet?

Let the ball bounce on —

carpet

wooden floor

bathroom tile

sidewalk

grass

gravel

How does the ball bounce on each different material?

What sounds does the ball make as it bounces

on different materials?

20

The ball bounces higher and more times on hard materials than on soft materials.

The ball makes different sounds when it bounces on different materials.

Put a ball on a table.

Make sure the ball does not move.

Now what can you do to make the ball roll?

Before you look at the next page, think of

as many ways as you can.

Roll another ball against the first one.

Snap a rubber band
against the ball.

Hit the ball with your hand.

Blow air against the ball.

Hit the table with your hand.

Lift one end of the table.

Can you think of any other ways to make the ball roll?

How can you use a ball to find out if a table is tipped or level?

Put a ball on the table. If the ball does not roll, the table is level.

If the ball rolls, the table is tipped.

The ball rolls the way the table is tipped.

Rest one end of the cardboard on a book.

Put a ball on the cardboard.

The ball rolls downhill.

What can you do to *stop* the ball from rolling?

Think of different ways.

Did you think of these ways?

Put a heavy block in front
of the ball.

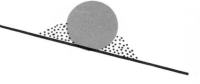

Put the ball on a
little pile of salt.

Glue the ball to
the cardboard.

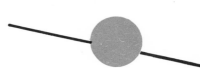

Make a hole in the cardboard
and put the ball in it.

Wrap a string around
the ball and attach the string
to the cardboard.

What other way
did you do it?

Get an old ball.

Ask your father to put a hole in the ball.

Put the hole near your cheek.

Squeeze the ball hard.

What happens?

A wind blows against your cheek.

Air is squeezed out.

There is air inside the ball.

Do you see why a ball is an interesting thing?

It is round.

It is a sphere.

It springs back when it is squeezed and let go.

It bounces.

It rolls.

It contains air.

It shows if things are level.

What else can YOU find out about a ball?

Think of what YOU want to do. Try it.

See what YOU can discover.